Short Passages

Caleb Gattegno

Educational Solutions Worldwide Inc.

First published in the United States of America in 1968. Reprinted in 1974.
Reprinted in 2010.

Educational Solutions Worldwide Inc.
2nd Floor 99 University Place, New York, N.Y. 10003-4555
www.EducationalSolutions.com

Table of Contents

1 Peter's Beach

In front of the house there was a beach. Peter liked to stretch on the sand when the sun was warming it. From the back door of the house he would walk along a path as far as the sand, and stand at the water's edge looking at the sea. When nothing very interesting was happening on the water, he would go down on his knees and take a handful of sand. Through his fingers ran the sand till only small stones and shells were left. Then with a large sweep of his arm and with as much strength as he could muster Peter would throw them away as far as he could.

At other times he would go on his back and gaze up at the clouds, his hands idly searching the sand at his sides. He never stopped playing with the sand and feeling it run through his fingers, however much he was absorbed by the changes in the clouds.

Occasionally some fishing boats came close enough to the beach for Peter to see what the fishermen were doing. Then with his hands clasped he would look and look, while his whole body moved with the boat from side to side. When the fishermen drew in their nets or cast them into the water, Peter would do the same with an imaginary net of his own from his place on the beach.

On the small beach Peter had a world of his own.

2 The Impatient Customer

The watchmaker, his magnifying glass on his left eye, was busy repairing a small watch for a customer who was leaving the town in an hour's time. He did not hear the doorbell ring as the door opened and closed. Now in the shop waited a big man who wanted to be attended to but nobody came to serve him. After a few minutes the man became impatient and called out loudly: "Anybody there?" The watchmaker jumped in his seat and the tool he was holding fell to the floor and shot beneath a heavy cupboard. He looked up and saw that the man was nearly angry; he looked down to see if he could spot his tool, still keeping his magnifying glass on his eye. When he looked up again he realized unhappily that he would have to give up his task and try to serve the big angry man.

It was not his job to attend to customers, his job was to repair watches. But his uncle who ran the shop had been called away without saying when he would be back.

The watchmaker rose slowly from his seat to go to the counter where the big man stood looking fiercely at him. He was as white as a sheet, and with his magnifying glass looked like a one-eyed snail. Neither spoke, but much was thought by both of them. The little watchmaker wished the big man had not come to trouble him in his work. The big man, not wanting this snail-man to serve him, leaned forward over the counter as if to grab him. The watchmaker took two steps back to escape his grasp.

All this took only a few seconds and then the big man changed his mind, turned round and went, leaving the door open, the bell ringing and the little watchmaker baffled, motionless and unable to think what to do next.

3 A Rest by the Fire

Judith sat in the armchair near the fireplace and sighed with relief. At last she was home, near a good warm fire where the flames danced in the dark, and could forget all she had lived through during the day. She looked at the hearth where the logs were burning blue flames, while the coal at the sides threw up yellowish tongues that licked the walls and the other black chunks yet to catch fire. Though Judith preferred the yellow flames, the blue ones went with the crackling of the logs and the grey bark that seemed nearer her mood. They gave all that heat, all that life to the room but would burn out soon in a crumbling destiny to be heard in the collapsing of the logs. Judith felt so in sympathy with the logs, musing on all she had been doing during the day with the agitation that made people believe she was lively, active, efficient, perhaps even interested whilst, in her heart, she knew she too was wasting her energy, just burning herself out like the logs: for whom she did not know—or care much.

The capricious dancing flames, the height they reached, the warmth they radiated, the mysterious beauty of the fire all at once took hold of Judith's dream. She felt protected, cozy in her armchair, in her room, happy to do nothing but feel that she was there and herself. Sleep came and she drowsed in the chair, nodding until her head rested on her shoulder for support. A new dream started; one that she could no longer direct upon the rhythm of the dancing flames and their colors, a true dream of the tired girl she was.

When she awoke she found only ashes where the logs had been; no more blue flames, only a deep redness in the centre of the hearth among the quietly burning coals. She felt hungry and cold, got up quickly to become the efficient, active person who would in no time prepare a satisfying dinner for herself.

4 The Hoped-for Meeting

The shy man was waiting for the girl behind a tree. She was getting ready to go to her friend's house on the other side of the wood and did not think anything would happen to her on the way. The man was waiting and thinking: "She can't be very long now." A few minutes later the girl appeared at the far end of the lane. She could not see the man, though he could see her clearly and was getting ready to come out and talk to her. She came closer and closer to him.

He felt something different every moment, one moment he knew he would come out and talk to her, the next he feared that he might frighten her and make her angry with him. When she was practically level with the tree, he made himself long and thin so that she did not see him as she passed by.

He held his breath for a full minute till she was out of sight at the other end of the lane, then he sat down at the foot of the tree not knowing what he was doing or why.

5 "I Don't Believe You"

"I don't believe you," said Guy to his friend, who was telling him an incredible story about himself.

"Why? Have you never even heard of these things?" replied Jimmy who loved to pull people's legs.

"How could you expect me to believe that?" said Guy heatedly, "I'm not a fool you know."

"Well let's forget it and find a place to sit down."

Guy was ready to forget what Jimmy had told him but was not ready to forgive him for the insult of thinking that he was stupid, or that he could be so easily fooled.

Jimmy knew very well that he might have hurt Guy's feelings and his pride, but his sense of humor was such that he continued as if his story was true and he was prepared to stand by it, pretending he thought whoever would not believe it was a fool. In fact, Jimmy's apparent pity for the poor fellow beside him infuriated Guy, who wanted to hold Jimmy to account. The more Jimmy seemed to sneer, the more Guy became upset and unable to find the right words to say.

So Jimmy said: "Do you see that path there? It must lead to a picnicking spot near the river. Let's go there and rest for a bit. I'll tell you another story like the one you are still thinking about when we've finished our sandwiches."

Guy could not control himself any longer: "I am not thinking of your story . . . I do not want you to tell me another one . . . I think you are vulgar and inconsiderate . . . that you tell lies to show off . . . that you . . ." Guy turned round and strode quickly away from Jimmy who, though pleased with the effect on his friend, was sorry to be left to eat his lunch by himself.

He watched Guy disappear round a bend some distance away and said to himself: "How can mere words have such power to make people angry and unhappy?"

6 The Deer's Antlers

Sitting in the waiting room, John examined with close attention a deerskin and some antlers which hung on the wall opposite.

"How could you tell just by looking whether the skin and the antlers belonged to the same animal?" John wondered. His knowledge was not sufficient even for him to be sure whether they belonged to a red deer or a reindeer, an antelope or some other animal of the same family. Now why had he been so quickly satisfied when first saying to himself: "This is a deerskin"? Was it because of visits to the zoo a few years earlier?—or because of a picture in a zoology book or a dictionary? He lacked the certainty that settles such matters in one's mind, for he had no clear image of opening a book somewhere, or of a visit to a zoological garden which would bring back reality. But as he searched his experience he remembered a film he had seen years earlier and the whole story came back vividly and conclusively. It was a film about wild life in Northern Canada and much of it was devoted to deer and their behavior.

Having settled this point, John got up from his chair and went to the wall to touch the skin and observe the antlers from closer. The skin gave him a strange feeling. From a distance it looked velvety and smooth, but when he ran his fingers over the hair it felt stiffer than he expected. Because of this it seemed unusually hard, even prickly. He tried to imagine why these animals had such hair, reliving the northern winter and the icy breezes of the film. With so little experience to go on, he left the topic for a moment, returning to the possibility of having one dead animal in front of him in the two objects he could touch.

The antlers were just too high for John to touch unless he stood on tiptoe and stretched his arm right out. His fingers first felt the dust left on the antlers from the last cleaning and, leaving aside his first thought, he touched with his thumb and two fingers the base of one of the antlers, near the wood to which they were glued. Fully stretched against the wall, his cheek rubbing against the skin, he was trying to feel better what was under his fingers when a door opened behind him and the nurse said, "Would you come in, Mr. Smith . . ."

7 The Four Players

The four players used to meet once a week round the bridge table. They enjoyed each other's company and rarely quarreled, though sometimes their tempers ran high if a partner made a silly mistake. They became so used to each other's play that they were reluctant to invite outsiders, except perhaps close friends or relatives who chanced to be in the locality—but then only to watch silently. As holiday time approached, they would consult very carefully about dates and intentions, arranging to go all to the same place or cancelling the weekly meeting. In this way they kept the date while on holiday, or else avoided having to invite an outsider.

Tonight the game was gloomy since one of the players had announced that his boss had offered him promotion to assistant manager, on condition that he move to a distant branch of the firm. The other three players knew that his quandary was theirs too. They spoke often of their progress at their jobs, knowing that each was happy to be promoted, and they had celebrated each occasion round this very table. But promotion had never before interfered with the most important event of the week: bridge.

Their eyes were on their cards but their minds were on these extraordinary circumstances for which they had no explanation: how could promotion be so disruptive? If he agreed to go away, he would lose their company and they might decide to bring in a 'stranger'—which had so far been an intolerable thought. The alternative would be to give up the meetings altogether.

Could he refuse to be promoted and stay put? Would that create a precedent, forcing each to give up hope of improving his position?

These thoughts were worrying and the bids required by the game in progress lacked altogether the usual luster and verve of imaginative bridge players: tonight the game reflected their gloomy state of mind. Then one of them remarked that he did the Sunday paper bridge problem every week and asked if anyone else looked at it? One answered, yes: one said, occasionally and the fourth volunteered that he had tried it once but had found it dull. The game stopped for a few minutes while they considered the pros and cons of newspaper bridge problems. The player who enjoyed them and found in them challenges that stretched his ability attempted to bring the others to share his enthusiasm.

During their previous meetings the game itself had occupied all their attention. Tonight for the first time, one player's problem freed them all to talk of other topics and they began to enjoy each other's company for something more than the rubber of bridge. This exchange of ideas, while still about bridge their common interest, was now leading to something else. Their acquaintance through the card games, their own good nature and their mutual respect were reaching out towards other areas, in which was working the unspoken intimacy of regular confrontations of their whole selves, each engaged in doing the best with what chance put in his cards. Unchecked by good manners and the card game, they were finding each other as true friends and were prepared to discuss not just the merits and demerits of published bridge problems but also their problems of promotion, and more.

The cards lay untouched on the table, the evening advanced and midnight struck at the big tower clock. Even though no solution had been proposed which would make them all happy—including the director who had proposed the move—something more important had happened. The player could go back to his employer and talk to him seriously now that the four of them had given the matter so much thought. To stay or to move was no longer like tossing a coin.

8 The Strike Avoided

Of all the pupils in his class Trevor was the only one the teacher disliked. From the day school reopened and Trevor entered the classroom the clash was inevitable. The teacher could not accept Trevor's speech and Trevor did not see why he should change it. At home and in his street everyone talked like him and nobody ever said: "You either keep quiet or speak as we do." He found this most unfair and often talked aloud, which resulted in immediate and unavoidable punishment. His parents did not dare visit the school to speak to the teacher, in spite of Trevor's begging them to. They believed the teacher must have good reasons for asking Trevor to change his way of talking, though they could not really see what all the fuss was about.

As time went by Trevor became bolder, no longer caring when he was punished. One day he made up his mind to ask all his schoolmates during break to go on strike if the teacher did not stop picking on him. They did not mind his accent or his vocabulary: they liked his friendliness, his jokes and several of the new games he taught them which he had learnt in the streets

17

near his home. But they were not prepared at first to go on strike as he asked because they did not know what a strike was. So he explained what he had heard people say in his neighborhood: "They said one day: 'If the people above you do not take you into account you all stop working and put your hands in your pockets for an hour or two during working time. Then you do it again the next day and the day after until you get what you want.'" Trevor went on: "It's easy to go on strike. Can't you all sit on your hands and keep quiet when the teacher wants you to work?"

They all agreed it was easy. But they could not at once agree when to strike. They told him they would think about it and give him an answer after the weekend. Trevor was happy in his new role as a leader and when he got back to his desk everyone in the class was looking at him. He suddenly seemed much bigger, much stronger than before. So intent were they all on him and so happy was Trevor that the teacher suspected something and called him to his desk. As never before, Trevor walked proudly forward with his head up and his step firm. The teacher for the first time noticed that not everything about him was objectionable. He was struck by the manly manner of the boy and instead of telling him off as usual, asked gently: "Trevor, do you think that as strong a boy as you could lift this desk?" Trevor, surprised, did not answer but turned round, gathered his strength, lifted the desk onto his back and walked a few steps carrying it.

Teacher and class were full of admiration and forgot to tell him to put the desk down, so Trevor kept it on his back for a little while longer. Then the teacher helped him to put it down and said: "Show me your tongue—is it as big and heavy as this desk?" Trevor and the class laughed but the teacher continued: "Do you think you can manage your tongue as easily as you managed your whole body when you picked up this desk?" Trevor did not quite understand so the teacher explained: "Now Trevor, try to say the following word like I do, and don't let your tongue beat you." Trevor said it correctly almost at once, where before he had not succeeded because he had never tried. The class broke into applause and the teacher said, "Now say this . . . and this . . . and this . . ." Trevor did well in every case without hesitation.

So the game went on. In that lesson Trevor managed to correct his hearing and his saying of a large number of words which the teacher had been trying to correct from the first day. So pleased to see that entirely by chance he and the boy could at last cooperate, the teacher smiled often and talked kindly to him. The whole class co-operated too: they either crossed their arms or applauded Trevor while the teacher concentrated on him alone for a whole hour.

Trevor at one stage saw all his schoolmates with their arms folded, and remembered his talk to them . . . so now they were on strike and he was getting redress for all the wrongs he had suffered. Now the teacher called for his attention and got it at once for the next exercise, and the next, and the next.

On his way home that day Trevor heard his own voice saying most of what he'd uttered during the lesson, but instead of being angry as usual he was doing his best to pronounce the words as he had heard the teacher do.

Trevor believed he had got what he wanted through the help of his classmates and his strike. But the next day they told him that since all was well again there was no need for a strike. Trevor stopped dead, his eyes looking far away and his mind trying to understand why the teacher was suddenly so friendly, gave him so much attention and was so pleased with him.

9 Dangerous Crossing

In the brook there were some stepping-stones which were always used by people wanting to cross over. The brook could be torrential after rain and it was not easy to save oneself if one fell in its waters.

The children had been well disciplined so far. Their leader was ten-year old Robert, a Cub who loved the country and enjoyed long exploratory walks alone or with other Cubs, or with his father. He had learned to be careful, to listen to all sorts of noises, to notice everything on his path; to stop and think before acting in unknown areas.

It was summer, and the holidays had brought to the same camping site a number of children who became friends at once and started playing together. Their parents were very pleased because the children would enjoy their holidays more, but also because they themselves would have some peace to rest and be with each other.

Robert at once became the children's leader. He was by no means the tallest nor the strongest physically, but he knew so much about the countryside and could do so many useful things that all the children looked to him for expedition plans, for information on how to time their outings and how to prepare themselves according to distance and the weather. Robert was confident about most points raised by his new friends, but when unsure he would not answer till the following meeting. In between he would consult his father.

This was the ninth outing, the last but one before the families returned to their homes all over the country. Looking at a map of the area Robert had found that beyond the brook there was an ancient Roman camp, and he and his friends had agreed to go there. As usual, all had been carefully planned and everyone in the party knew exactly what to do in all imaginable situations. Only one thing was still uncertain, and that was the crossing of the brook. Robert had not explored it on his own because it was too far off to go there and come back in a short time. So he decided to risk it, only warning the party that they should sit at the brook for him to issue instructions which were to be observed very strictly. The night before, he talked things over with his father who, explaining the main dangers and how to avoid them, told him particularly how to look after the younger members of the party.

When they arrived on the bank the brook looked narrow, but its water rushed noisily between the stones. The foam on the surface hid the bottom in places and it was not easy to judge whether the water was three or six feet deep. Few of the children had yet learned to swim, though Robert himself had taken his first life-saving test. So he thoughtfully surveyed the steppingstones where a crossing was possible. He asked the others to sit down on the bank while he jumped from stone to stone to reach the other side.

It looked so easy that all were on their feet ready to follow him. But he shouted quickly: "Stop! Sit down! We aren't going any further." He returned to the party and said: "I'm sorry to disappoint you but I don't think we can let everybody risk the crossing because the water is too deep and anyone who slips will be drowned. The stones are slippery and we'd better go back to camp."

A loud protest followed his words. "If you can do it twice why can't we? Who do you think you are?" cried the bigger boys. Robert was now facing his first crisis as a leader, and he did not know what to do. He asked: "And if Jeremy, who is the smallest of us, falls in the water, who will go and rescue him? You, Alan; you Paul; you Richard? Yet you say you can't swim? If I have to try and save any of you and fail, or if I get drowned too, what would you tell my parents then?"

Robert's words seemed to accuse them all. Embarrassed and unhappy, the children saw themselves in the awful situation he described. But the attraction of visiting the Roman camp was still great and they tried to argue with him.

Robert knew the dangers existed, but he knew too that it could not be so very dangerous to cross the brook just there, for otherwise there would have been a notice to warn people. He was about to give in.

Fortunately for the children, a party of adults arrived at that moment, on their way to the Roman camp. They helped everybody across the brook that had once seemed so wide and difficult but, now they were across, so narrow and easy.

On the return journey the children were tired and when they reached the brook alone the thoughts of the morning came back. They sat looking at the noisy torrent and imagining all the dangers of which Robert had spoken. They refused to move and Robert now had to face a new crisis. He carefully stepped over the stones and reached the other side in a few moments. Returning, he told Alan to take his shoes off and cross over, giving him his hand. The water and the stones were icy cold but Alan safely reached the other bank. One after the other the children took off their shoes and were helped by Robert to step carefully over the stones until they reached the right side. When all had crossed, Robert returned to collect the shoes. So many pairs! He took his own first and threw them across the water. Seeing that they landed safely, he sent the others by the same route. All the shoes except one of Alan's reached the other side well beyond the wet bank. Alan, prompted by the thought of walking back bare-footed, quickly stretched his hand into the water and rescued the shoe a second before it sank in the foaming waters.

The journey home was silent and uneventful except that Alan, who felt his cold, wet shoe on one foot, slowed down the pace of the party.

No-one forgot Robert's good leadership, neither on their last day together nor on the following vacations, though they never met again.

10 The Wily Fish

Day after day he came to the same place to fish and day after day he went home without a catch. His wife would marvel why everybody could find fish except him. She asked him to tell her where he went and what he found there. He told her that the place was full of fish, big ones that seemed game and very good eating, with enough left over to make soup for later. But they would not bite.

His wife suggested that they should go together next day, and he agreed. The place was excellent from all points of view: there were stones to sit on, the shade of the trees tempered the heat of the sun and helped create an atmosphere of peace and contentment that would attract any angler. The water was clear and many fish were cruising by.

The fishing tackle was prepared. The best bait hid a sharp hook and the line was almost new. The man asked his wife whether she would like to throw the line, as he had done it so often before. She agreed and cast so well that the bait landed amongst the largest fish swimming near the bank. Both watched with their eyes wide open, picturing the scene they anticipated. But nothing happened. The fish seemed most contemptuous of the bait. They would even come close up to the hook, as if smelling the bait and despising it. Then, one after the other, they would turn round and go.

If from the bank the anglers tried to hook any fish, they only plunged down together, leaving the bait dangling alone in the empty water.

This comedy of the contemptuous fish enraged the wife, while it had so far only puzzled the husband. She fired a hundred questions at him about hooks, baits, places on the banks, leads, lines and the weather. He had studied them all and could find no fault with the material side of the affair, so he suggested that perhaps these were super-intelligent fish, the élite of the species who knew a great deal about fishermen and taught their young to be careful and watchful so no-one could catch them.

His wife was deeply moved by this thought and went straight to town to tell her friends about the super-intelligent fish in the pond. They all wanted to see for themselves and long queues of people formed, waiting till the man and his wife came to fish and then watching them catch nothing.

When all their friends had told all *their* friends about them, the people of neighboring towns started coming, and still longer queues formed, earlier in the morning, until people started queuing a week in advance to see the angling couple as they tried in vain to catch one of these super-intelligent fish.

A year went by. The anglers tried in all weathers and at all hours of the day, but failed to catch a single fish in that pond. One day a visiting fisherman sat down on the other side and threw his line with an ordinary bait on an ordinary hook among the fish that seemed only to sneer at our friends' attempts to catch them. Not a minute later, he hooked an enormous fish and at the next cast, and the next, and the next he caught more of these huge creatures that the long queues of people had been admiring for their intelligence.

Filling his basket in less than twenty minutes, he left the place and walked along the bank while the onlookers, baffled by what they saw on either side, asked themselves who was pulling whose leg.

The angler and his wife moved to the other side and cast their line, at once hooking an enormous fish. They continued for a few minutes and got as many more as they wanted.

The story was told in the national press. The Royal Society sent its most celebrated specialists to investigate the strange happenings witnessed by so many citizens.

11 The Hermit and his Friends

On the mountainside there was a hut sheltered from the prevailing winds by the rocks that served as one of its walls. The rest of the hut had been built by one man, a hermit who spent several months in the work that was to provide him with shelter and the solitude he was seeking.

The mountain was not one of the highest in the chain, but it was rugged and difficult to climb, so mountaineers were discouraged from attempting it and the hermit was assured of some peace. At last he had managed to cut himself off from other men.

Animals did not disturb him. He even managed to make friends with some of them. In particular a big bear became fond of him and would come at noon to the entrance of the hut and sit outside looking at the hermit inside, meditating. He would remain silent till the hermit moved and made him the sign that meant: come in now.

The empty hut was as much a home for the bear as it was for the man. On the ground in a corner some pine cones with their seeds, and some acorns, formed the reserves of food. The bear would visit the corner and touch the food but would not eat any. A grunt of approval showed when the freshness of the food suited him, but he would turn his back in disgust if it had been there for some time.

Then the bear and the hermit would sit in front of the entrance and look at the mountain range and dream together at the sight of all this vast beauty. The feeling of complete independence, of complete self-sufficiency and of belonging to the immensity, at one with nature, would send the hermit back to his meditation and the bear to its forest for a few more days.

Occasionally on a bright day an antelope would manage the climb to the hut and venture lightly onto the platform of rocks near the entrance. On these occasions the hermit came out at once and held the shy animal's head against his breast, feeling a fellowship of a kind he could not have with the bear. The antelope, with no movement of fear, let him show his affection and accept it as something natural. This contact with the antelope threw the hermit back upon his thoughts about mankind and the brotherhood of men which he was beginning to realize for himself.

In no time the antelope would disappear into the woods below, leaving behind a trail of grace to fill the eye of the solitary man for a few days.

When storm-clouds surround the hut, like a laboratory where the lighting, the ozone in the air, the thunder and torrential rain create a menacing, frightening atmosphere, a black eagle sometimes calls on the hermit. He does not go beyond the entrance to the hut, and the hermit does not move from his place. A silent, intense dialogue takes place; the eagle with one eye on the man and one on nature covering two realms at once, the hermit completely taken by the majesty of this powerful master of space, who seizes any change in the landscape for miles around. The eagle always seems to wonder when he comes: how does this extraordinary creature share in the management of *my* space? Yet he always leaves without an answer for the hermit remains silent in his contemplation of his visitor till the eagle plunges like an arrow through a hole in the clouds and down into the space below.

The hermit's friends have not yet been introduced to each other. 'Will this ever happen?' is a question on which he often meditates.

12 The Concert

After queuing for hours, they were at last admitted and found standing-room behind a pillar in the gallery. The famous conductor and orchestra were appearing in the town for three concerts only, so many people wanted to be in the theatre to hear them even though the concerts were to be broadcast. That evening was the last, and the orchestra's reputation was even higher than on the first day.

There was some time before the concert started and our friends looked down into the theatre as so many others were doing. In the stalls, the expensive seats, there were still a number of empty places, most likely reserved for well-to-do people who would arrive a few moments before the concert began and force long rows of the audience to get up and let them pass. Indeed this was already happening: the first two seats of one row, especially, were occupied for a while and then came other couples or individuals whose seats were immediately next to those just taken. To the people above, these increasing rows of people bobbing up and down made a sight as interesting and amusing as the filling up of the orchestra seats by the musicians.

The musicians came in, opened their music, tuned their instruments, chatted with a companion, and the tiers of seats on the sides of the hall began to fill up too. In the boxes, ladies in fur coats took the front seats, leaving their escorts to help them off with their coats and hand them their gilt opera glasses before themselves sitting at the back of the box.

Particularly striking to onlookers from above was the large number of bald heads among the better-off members of the audience who sat in the front stalls and the boxes. The lights reflected on their shiny surfaces made it harder not to notice them.

The theatre was almost full by the time the leader of the orchestra entered. He was soon followed by the conductor. The air was stuffy already and delicate throats were being cleared. Coughs of all kinds and at all pitches could be heard, as if people wanted to make sure that they at any rate would not disturb the performance.

The leader received a great ovation from all parts of the hall, especially from the gallery, but the conductor seemed even more popular for he had to wait several minutes until the applause died down before he could begin. Most of the audience knew his work, and this was enough to make them enthusiastic. The concert opened with the National Anthem, but at the end of the first piece on the program, the audience seemed still more excited for a fraction of a second after the last note, as if listening had bottled up their powers, their applause exploded and lasted for interminable minutes. The conductor bowed this way and that, turning to the leader and the orchestra so that all would know that the players too had taken part in the performance and deserved the congratulations. Some people must have felt a little embarrassed for the conductor, who could neither leave his place nor go on with the program. Still, such was the excitement caused by the music that they needed to let off steam somehow.

And so the concert went on. Some people were quite unable to control their coughing and could not help irritating their neighbors as they punctuated the lovely music with sounds which were in no way intended by the composer or the orchestra. Only at the occasional pauses in the concert was it permissible to loosen one's throat and fill the theatre with explosions which had been strictly controlled during the performance.

Some people must have suffered, even while listening to this fine music, for the ventilation was clearly insufficient and many seats were badly placed. Yet no one present would have missed the concert for worlds; neither the stuffy air nor the struggle with one's chest and throat would count against these hours lived under the spell of such magicians and such creators of music.

13 Evelyn's New Dress

This was the first party at which Evelyn had worn her new dress. She was only fifteen and her mother had needed some persuading before buying so expensive a model. But there Evelyn stood, proud and smiling, happy to show off to her friends.

All the girls complimented Evelyn on her new dress and said they wished their own were so nice. The boys just looked, admiring the girl's figure rather than the dress which they hardly knew how to appreciate. A little overwhelmed, Evelyn was not sure whether to be more pleased by the looks from the boys or the compliments from the girls.

There was space for dancing in the middle of the large room. In one corner a record-player was playing the latest in pop music; in another was the buffet. A few chairs here and there against the wall were still empty for the party was just starting and nobody wanted to sit down yet.

The host and hostess were cousins and took it in turns to play master and mistress of ceremonies. Their job was to select records to please everybody, and the floor was occupied sometimes by solemn couples dancing the blues, sometimes by the whole party when the music was more exciting and sometimes by a rowdy group when the rhythm was really wild. After a few dances, groups formed according to like interests. Evelyn and three or four others formed a party on their own. Better dressed than the others, they avoided games that might spoil their clothes. Another group was formed by the rowdy boys and girls who enjoyed pulling each other's hair or ties or shoelaces and took great delight in putting ice cubes down the backs of each other's shirts or blouses. Other groups had different ideas of how to enjoy themselves.

The buffet was opened and those who were not dancing were invited to serve themselves. The rowdy group was unfortunately first at the table. Hungry and thirsty, they were not much concerned with the others and in no time most of the best food was on their plates and taken away. They even found time for second helpings before the hosts noticed the ravages and stopped the music so that the rest of the party could get some food.

What a sight for the better-mannered guests! The carefully-prepared trays of sandwiches, hors d'oeuvres and salads were in disorder and nearly empty: the scraps that remained did not look so appetizing, either. But there was enough for everyone to have at least something to eat and luckily there was enough fruit-juice left for them all to refresh themselves.

On their way back to their chairs, Evelyn and her group commented quietly on the bad manners of the others, agreeing that it was a shame for the hosts to be left with so little. To avoid a cushion lying on the floor, Evelyn saw that she would have to push someone or else lose her balance. The girl whose arm she jogged was holding a glass of fruit-juice, which slipped from her fingers and fell onto the carpet. Instantly the girl's dress, that of another girl, the cushion and the carpet were all splashed with fruit-juice and stained. Evelyn could not believe it was she who had caused so much damage. Upset and ashamed, she was nevertheless glad that her own dress had not suffered in the havoc. The two girls who had been splashed did not share her discomfort but quickly asked for a wet cloth and some soap to clean up the mess, and for somewhere to dry their clothes. Everyone helped, except Evelyn and her group who in their embarrassment did not know what to do.

Evelyn finished her food and drink, apologized to everyone and then went home. The two girls borrowed dressing-gowns from their hostess and the party continued as gaily as before.

14 The Joys of Speed

The car was speeding along as if it was the only one on the road. The two young men in it liked to drive fast and to pass as many other cars as possible. They were very sorry when they could not overtake and thought only of getting the fastest car in the world.

At home their parents would tell them their behavior was dangerous not only to themselves but also to other people who happened to be on the road at the same time. But the two young men thought only of their dream. Luckily, by taking turns to drive they learnt a great deal about driving fast and yet carefully: but driving fast is always dangerous and it was not easy to be sure of avoiding an accident. Yet in months of driving they had never caused an accident, nor had they let others force them into one.

In the driving mirror they noticed that they were being followed closely by a car with two men in the front seats and three in the back. It was a powerful car which could go much faster than our young men's, yet at no time did it overtake. It only followed them, as closely as was safe. When they stopped to get petrol, the black car stopped too. As they got out, the five men came straight up to them and surrounded them. They were five big, strong men and our friends immediately thought they were plain-clothes policemen.

The man who had been sitting next to the driver spoke first: "We've been watching you for some days now. You seem to enjoy driving at top speed and beating every other driver on the road."

"But we've always kept within the speed limit—and followed the Highway Code," said one of the young men, sure now that he was talking to the police.

"Yes, I must say, you may drive fast, but you do seem to have good road sense."

"We've never caused anyone any trouble, though I expect we've irritated a good many other drivers."

"Let me introduce myself. My name is Mason—TTB racing drivers' coach."

"Are you?!" cried the two young men together, thrilled at meeting this important man face to face.

"This is Mr. Smith . . . Mr. Price . . . Mr. Hughes . . . Mr. McPherson, whom you must know by name. They are coaches of different racing clubs."

"Sure, we know you by name. We're honored . . ."

"Well," said Mr. Mason, "We are always on the look-out for keen, careful drivers. We need more and more people to train up to international racing standards. We all think you are worth giving a chance."

"How old are you?" asked Mr. McPherson.

"Both over twenty-one—though he is only just over."

"What would your parents say if you told them you were going to train to be professional racing drivers?"

"They may be upset, but I'm sure they would not stand in our way."

"Hm," said Mr. Mason again, "You talk it over with each other and your parents and let me know. Here's my card with the address and telephone number. Good luck!"

"Thanks Mr. Mason, thank you, gentlemen!" cried the two, full of excitement. The five men went back to their car, the two young drivers stayed where they were for a while watching the black car reversing and then swiftly accelerating down the road.

The petrol pump attendants came over to them and the oldest said: "Congratulations! You must be good to be offered a chance like that. First time it's happened in *this* garage."

At home, their mother was not at all pleased. "Why should these people tempt our sons like this? The life of a racing driver is full of danger and risk: why can't our children get jobs like everyone else and drive for pleasure as they do now!"

But their father thought differently. "You can see how crazy they are about driving—they only talk of cars and beating everyone. The race tracks must be safer than the roads, simply because only very good drivers are allowed on them. I think they should accept and be trained by Mr. Mason while it is still possible."

"Oh, you always take the boys' side. You have beautiful arguments to support them. If they accept, I shall have to go and watch them train and see that nothing happens to them."

"But mother, you can't do that! No drivers' mothers are allowed in at the training track. Everybody knows why—if we're considered good enough, it's because they think we know exactly what is going on and how to look after ourselves. Don't forget that X . . . died in his bed covered with glory as most famous drivers do."

It was clear from the start of their training that these two men were in a class of their own and could expect to win many races all over the world.

15 Friends Without Speech

A great scholar, she had reflected deeply on the most profound themes. He too was a scholar who could speak with understanding on almost any subject. They lived under the same roof, but what a waste that they could communicate only on the most trivial matters! They appreciated what they knew of each other's work but the absence of proper verbal channels made the sharing of experience in an explicit way seem a challenge that was altogether beyond them.

Their feeling of waste lasted for some time until each discovered that this reflection and ability to study anything outside themselves left the heart of the problem untouched. How can two people full of goodwill and mutual concern reach one-another beyond words? Lovers live the illusion of communication without words through the elaborate language of love. But if two people do not choose to use this language, are all doors closed?

For some time he and she considered this new problem independently, and each came to the same conclusion. If we are to communicate what we ourselves know in order to be known by others, then it is necessary to use words. But if our own experience has any effect on our being, this will show and can be expressed through all our everyday gestures and actions. Is knowledge therefore to be put in words only, or can it show itself in one's way of being?

True, something is lost when we cannot communicate symbols which, by their own power, find their way into another's consciousness, there to effect their work. But surely something is also lost in overlooking the working of symbols on oneself before revealing it to others.

Knowledge is attractive for itself and one seems smaller if one has but little of it. People value less someone who cannot display enough knowledge, so it is cultivated by many as a social value, something that makes a person more worthwhile. The two scholars had also pursued it for these reasons but now that they could not communicate it, they wondered if it really was a value.

To each other they seemed civilized, good mannered, courteous; but was this the result of their knowledge and reflection, or was it the result of their upbringing and tastes? Where are the *visible* signs of knowledge, the signs that are not in the words?

It seemed likely that crises and periods of hardship would be better to show whatever wisdom had been gained from concentrated thinking about these absorbing subjects. Everyday experience calls as much for the common sense of ordinary people as for that of specialists. He and she were now waiting for the crises that might arise to test the truth of their new reflection.

16 Mark and Teresa

In their class were a few boys and girls who were much more interested in each other than in what the teacher had to offer. Mark and Teresa were two who believed they had fallen in love. Teresa was slim and pretty: Mark would try to look elegant, paying a great deal of attention to his appearance. He went to the hairdresser every week, bought shirts and trousers and would change his style often while most of his friends were content to wear the same outfit for some time.

Teresa wanted Mark to look after her and for ever to be her squire. Mark accepted this when it satisfied his vanity, but would sulk and refuse to do what Teresa asked if he thought it would lower his self-esteem. At first glance, it seemed that these two young people, engaged in getting the best out of life, would find it easy to get on together. But life has its own ways of testing every one of us, however clever or happy we are. Teresa believed firmly that her good looks gave her some right over anyone who happened to admire her. Mark had yielded for a time, and this strengthened her belief until she came to expect everyone to accept her view of life unquestioningly. So she became very unhappy when quite naturally Mark once smiled back at a girl in the class who had begun to find him attractive.

Teresa was present in the lesson, but her mind was elsewhere. Pat's and Mark's exchange of smiles, surely part of the daily currency of the class, became for Teresa the most tormenting event. She felt betrayed, all her love and all her life in danger, and had to use all her self-control to hold back the tears and the cry of pain that accompanied her discovery of such meanness in the knight who had given her his promise.

Mark felt the terrific tension mounting in his neighbor. He knew the cause since, although his smile to Pat had contained an understanding of her interest in him, he would not admit this to Teresa. Their *sotto voce* conversation went on all through the lesson. Completely absorbed in her feelings of grief, Teresa saw her world reduced to Mark, Pat and herself, though her self-control prevented the teacher from noticing anything unusual. Mark tried to be self-righteous in his replies, refusing to consider himself a traitor—which was all Teresa wanted from him. He could have regained her confidence had he promised not to smile at Pat again, Pat who had suddenly become a rival to Teresa. Instead, he denied her the knowledge of what was going on inside him when he smiled. It hurt her most that the boy she liked best was refusing her the intelligence of the things of the heart, denying her sense of truth at work.

The lesson over, Teresa dragged Mark outside by the hand to the most isolated bench in the playground. Violently she poured out her grief, but succeeded only in bringing out the worst in him. His answers were sharp and unkind. His sympathy diminished every minute. Teresa hardly found it possible to go to the staff room and ask to be excused for the rest of the day.

At home she shut herself up in her room crying and swearing to give up Mark, yet crying for her love and wishing to forgive him if only . . .

Meanwhile Mark started courting Pat who at this moment seemed so much more attractive than Teresa.

17 The Value of Silence

During her sabbatical year, Connie went round the world. A teacher all her life and unmarried, she believed she was interested in people, in the cultures of the past and in seeing as much as she could of as many places as possible.

Her trip had indeed been full of events. She gathered so many anecdotes about characters and personages in the most extraordinary circumstances that, back home, she could keep large gatherings on tenterhooks while she told of her adventures. Everywhere she went, she was welcomed for the stories she could tell so well.

But Connie soon realized it was her stories, not herself, that people appreciated. She asked herself how she could define the boundary between one's own being and the experiences one goes through and is identified with. Were the happenings in Rome or Paris, in Katmandu and Benares, unique because of her, or could anyone live through them in just the same way as she did? What did interest others in her stories?

There was plenty for Connie to find out if she really wanted the best answers to her new preoccupations. Her next opportunity was at a gathering of intelligent people at a colleague's house. As usual, the conversation chanced to start anywhere. Some people talked of news in the evening papers; others about the coming local elections; others about their children and their illnesses; others about so-and-so who had found a post elsewhere and so on.

Connie for the first time watched what happens in such gatherings: how groups get together, all listening to one person or else finding a general topic in which everyone can take part. It was fascinating. The hostess seemed keen at first to let everyone talk of what they happened to find interesting, herself merely seeing that everyone was comfortable and had within easy reach something to eat and drink. But when all this had been taken care of, she could start thinking of the rest of the evening. Everyone was assessed for what she knew he or she could bring to the party.

"Obviously," thought Connie, "she will count on me as an entertainer, capable of telling good stories with enthusiasm and as they happened to me." But the hostess might also have something else up her sleeve. So Connie watched the people. Who among the guests had something to contribute to the evening? Did she know them well enough to be able to answer her own question? Clearly not: most of them she had met either casually before or not at all until that night. How could she believe that she had been invited because she had something to give? Perhaps everyone thought likewise of themselves—indeed anyone who could talk well of what happened to him during the day and reach some understanding of what mystery there is in almost everything would find many ready to listen, to share in the experience. Was it necessary to have gone far, to have seen strange places to move people: or did communication take place because people can be moved by any experience that adds to their own life?

Connie began to see that she was looking at people through colored spectacles, and that she had missed many chances of knowing persons for what they were because she became so involved in her own story of her idea of what she had lived through.

For once Connie kept silent and quietly enjoyed her own growth in the observation of people and of her own motives and pre-conceived ideas. The evening passed quickly. No one asked her specially about her trips, though many talked to her and, feeling she was inwardly inclined, respected her wish to communicate silently with all.

When she left she told her hostess sincerely how much she had enjoyed being there with her friends.

18 Snowfall

The house in the country was comfortable, well heated and beautifully appointed. From every point of view the rooms had something to offer. The roof beams, the stones and mantelpiece of the fireplace, the staircase, all created an impression of calculated simplicity that linked the present with the past. The comfort of the uniformly-spread warmth was modern, but the occupants of the house had intended to make it unobtrusive as if it came from nowhere. Occasionally they would light a fire of logs which would crackle and spread the scents of burning pine wood, but the real warmth still came from elsewhere.

Nature outside, withdrawn into itself, would make the lonely, comfortable house inaccessible to outsiders, or like a besieged fortress for the people in it.

One day a blizzard changed the world into a lovely white expanse, so beautiful to look at and to experience. The Christmas-card fir trees appeared heavy with their double load of green branches and white snow. Roofs lost their redness and showed more sharply their rectangular shapes which cut into the surrounding background of slopes and woods. The leafless trees told that the cold season had not yet gone and that more snow could be expected.

Only two or three days earlier the sun had shone, warming the walls and announcing the coming warm weather, the hot springs and summers of this altitude. The fields, now completely white again, had then taken on a green that was particularly vivid before the melting of the previous snows. Its contrast with the brown of the trees and the grey-blue skies went straight to one's heart and made one tender. The rolling fields gave a changing landscape which any visitor to the area would find attractive and inviting.

But snow also means isolation. Roads are covered and lost in the fields. Distances to inhabited places suddenly become enormous and one is unprotected and cut off. There is so much to clear that human effort seems in vain. The modern equipment that permits the clearing of main roads will come this way maybe in a few day's time: will the snow-ploughs be able to open the narrow road that leads to the house with its warmth and serenity?

The beauty of the countryside is still seen but does not reach the core of the mind. A barrier of anxiety has been built around the heart and cannot be loosened. Looking at the landscape, one sees that the roads have disappeared and cannot be followed in safety by a car: the comforting surface leading to other people and civilization is now covered and united with the ditches at its sides. To go becomes suddenly as hazardous as driving through fog.

How can so much beauty and the feeling it arouses be so diminished by rising anxiety? Yet man never really believes that the change he is now witnessing in the world cannot be reversed and he looks for signs of improvement.

The clouds are thinning. The sun may appear in its glory and in no time melt this mass of white, leaving behind only a view of the beautiful landscape and the memory of fears experienced. The sun is now the friend one feels for, invites to emerge, encourages and directs for one's own ends. The comforted heart scans the luminous sky, covered still with clouds but now promising the change desired.

19 The Observatory

The observatory on top of the hill was open to the public on Sundays and holidays.

In the old days there were very few visitors and the ordinary staff of the institution would find time to show round small groups. Research went on at a moderate pace; the instruments were venerable and not very useful in the competition of advanced scientific work. Not much money was available in the State budget for astronomy.

Now that space is so much in the news, visitors to the observatory are shocked at the look of the equipment. In their hearts the staff feel two very different tendencies. They would like to encourage visitors to voice stronger and stronger protests so that the Government would upgrade the establishment, but they know also that it is not that easy for people trained in earlier days to maintain, control and use the new equipment they so much want. New staff would have to be brought in who may be more competent, who may even make present limitations more obvious so that life in this quiet place would become intolerable.

One of the assistants believes his function in the observatory is to create vocations, leaving to those he may inspire the job of advancing knowledge: be it in this observatory, improved or not, or anywhere else. So he scans the skies with his telescopes and finds the beings his papers tell him should be there. He looks at them with love for he is one of those people who can extend his self beyond his immediate surroundings, establish a personal link with each star, planet or other heavenly being and feel the pulses of these animated dots in the sky. To look at Saturn is a particular fascination but he finds himself overwhelmed by the mystery of each speck of light he turns to.

Of course he knows all this is romantic and sentimental, but is it less true for all that? He knows that there is much more to modern astronomy: that spectroscopy, radioastronomy and satellites have changed the techniques, the amount of knowledge, the future of research. Still, to him the cosmos is *man's* habitat and one's first enjoyment of one's world is through the senses. Different people enjoy different things and so he approaches visitors always with the assumption that they may not share his enthusiasm for the beauty of galaxies no more than a dot in the field of vision.

What excitement for him to find every week at least one of the visitors sharing his understanding of the greatness of what is there to be seen! What good he has done just by directing people's eyes to some remarkable spot that bursts the boundaries of consciousness because now the actual and marvelous universe is open to our sensitivity! For him, this experience maintains the significance of his job in spite of all the handicaps he knows this approach to the universe may generate in the minds of future scientists. He asks himself: "What value to man is much knowledge if he loses the sense of mystery and the reverence for true greatness? Man's experience of the cosmos is a meeting with his future, not a catalogue of names and figures!"

But he keeps these thoughts to himself, and expresses them only in his preparations for the visits that will maybe open the way for a direct insight into the mysteries. The factual description of instruments is of lesser importance.

20 The Unsuspected Legacy

When they got married, they were young and full of ambition. They would spend long hours imagining their future house when life might permit them to fill it with the costly things needed to make it as comfortable and as beautiful as they desired. But one after the other children came, altering the priorities and preventing the house from becoming much more than a shelter. For it was obvious that the children's needs and their education were more important than a tiled bathroom or the most up-to-date stereophonic radiogram.

Nevertheless the dream had got hold of them to such an extent that to talk of it was a necessary substitute for putting their plans into practice. Most events at home would lead to it. The growing children would soon need a room each, which in turn required a house larger than the present one. Their increasing circle of friends and the need to entertain them all made the present house again an obstacle and the need for the next one imperative.

Slowly the children had been brought into the dream and they in turn pressed for the change, indicating the inadequacies of their present shelter. As time went by, the pressures building up in each member of the family became almost intolerable. The conversation between the parents was no longer full of hope, but impatient and almost always led to a stalemate: "How can we get the house we need if all we have is what we earn and spend!" No money meant no house. "Where does one get money?" was the form the pressure now took.

There are of course many ways of raising money, but so few seemed open to them. Saving was practically excluded on the present income. To earn a lot more would entail a change of employment for him and a job for her or the children. He had spent all his working life with one firm and to leave almost seemed a heresy. She had been a housewife for the same number of years and was little prepared for another type of life. To win the football pools, a lottery or a racing bet was attractive, but no-one has made a fortune here without being extremely lucky. Was this family lucky? Their own life seemed so far to prove the opposite. So to bet would be tempting the devil in oneself. To borrow would be the most normal thing to do, but how, given their existing securities, could they get the large loan needed? The idea of stealing could not be entertained even for a moment.

To inherit from an unknown relative would be so near the essence of the old dream that they preferred to think of this solution rather than all others.

The horizon seemed totally closed and all hope for the new house lost. Slowly this view became the only possible reality: the parents would wait until the children grew up and left home, then the house would be large enough and would cost less to run just for the two of them.

The day acceptance of this situation was complete, a cable told them of the death of an uncle they hardly knew and of his leaving them, among other things, his large property in the country with two years' running expenses.

21 At the Barber's

The whole row of chairs was occupied and all the barbers were occupied too. New customers opening the door, discouraged at seeing all the people waiting for a haircut, would leave despite the manager's assurances that it would not be long before they were attended to.

Up-to-date magazines were mixed with old ones which were still there for some reason. The waiting customers found it difficult to concentrate on their reading, so compelling were the topics discussed by the barbers and their customers.

Some preferred watching to reading, and would try to forecast whether they would get a better cut from this or that barber; whether bad luck would send them to the chair of this man who would so obviously make a mess of their hair. Luck and the number on your ticket decided whom you got in this hairdresser's, for people without an appointment could not choose their man.

The barbers would turn the chair away from the mirrors which covered one wall, as if they did not want their work constantly supervised by their customers. But they used the mirror as an aid rather than as a spy on their work and most of the time the customer would have his head down anyway, without worrying whether the hair at the back of the neck or the sides was being attended to.

The barbers used their tools in different ways. One, asked or unasked, would start working with his scissors at the sides. Another would take his clippers first and trim the back of the head; yet another would use clippers only for starting, and would then select a pair of scissors for each different job. One would comb your hair every few minutes and step back to consider the effect of his work before deciding what to do next. The customers too were very different: there were some who came because they had to—because hair will go on growing and must be cut from time to time. Their position did not permit them to look scruffy or romantic. There were those on the other hand who came as to an ally who would ease their task of impressing so and so in their favor. There were children too, brought by grown-ups.

Children over a certain age were asked to sit on a padded board across the arms of the chair. One little boy told his father he would not like this particular man to cut his hair; he wanted another one. Standing no nonsense his father lifted him onto the raised chair and told him not to be so awkward. But the barber knew a crying child is a difficult subject so started trying to win him over by talking kindly to him. What he said did not matter, but it seemed so funny and entertaining that the boy's objections were quite overcome and the father soon realized he had been angry for nothing. The child had not only forgotten the scene and the tension of a few moments ago, but was thoroughly enjoying the communication with this man in white who, in no time at all, had wrapped him in a nylon overall, got out his scissors and started trimming the crown of his head.

The waiting customers once more counted the people whose turn was before their own. Perhaps some were only waiting for others, in which case the queue would move more quickly. The boy and his father misled them for when the boy was through, his father abruptly told him to wait quietly while he too had his hair cut.

22 Rare Books

Every week John spent a few hours looking at books in some of the second-hand bookshops in this street. He was fond of reading but preferred not to go as far as the public library to see what he could find for his weekend reading. The second-hand bookshops had some very good bargains for knowledgeable people and John fancied himself to be one. Had he not spent twenty years looking for that rare book, or those first editions that had not been recognized as valuable by the bookseller?

Reading a first edition seemed to John a very different experience from that of reading later ones. Why? He would not be able to explain in so many words. In the kind of literature John had access to the text rarely differed much between editions, though he might find it greatly revised in scientific works. Yet the mere fact that it was a first edition he was holding, particularly one not noted as such, made John feel altogether different about the scanning of the lines and the pages. The words and the sentences were immersed in a secondary knowledge, a mental background that colored them and made them sound different.

John never knew really what to do with this new sense which he believed he had developed more than other readers and bookshop browsers, but he felt that something about his reading was enhancing his whole self. For him this did not lie only in sharing the content of the story, in the aesthetic experience of good writing, or even in the contact with great writers. There was a direct link with the book, the material book as a work of art. He could not fully forget, even while being thrilled by the adventures shared with the author, that the type, the layout, the quality of the paper, the feel of the whole book, its cover and weight—all were integral parts of the experience and helped or marred the absorption of the story. When he discovered a printing error on an otherwise immaculate page, he would feel a crime had been committed, particularly if the error made a word that distorted the meaning. The error would stick out like a sore thumb and the message would be reduced almost to nothing.

First editions are obviously greater carriers of errors, which can be noticed and corrected in later ones. This was one of the reasons why John would love to own first editions, so that he could feel *he* would not have let such an error pass, and could feel somehow superior to the printers' and publishers' readers by spotting what they had missed. By developing this trait John was in a way unfair to himself, for he would have saved himself some pain by purchasing later editions of the work he liked to read. This did not fully escape him but he explained it to himself by putting it low on his list of reasons for wanting first editions. Indeed rare books are more often than not first editions and his rare books could be sold at higher prices than later editions if ever he had to sell them for some urgent need.

Then again, first editions are the product of the publishers' planning and designing. They teach you something of the art which you may perhaps miss altogether when reading the same text as part of a reprint in a popular edition. Thirdly, John felt that an author may have had some say in the production of the first edition and that this interest matters: later, the author may be busy on something else and want above all to see his printed work selling well, agreeing to whatever the publisher proposes for this end. Authors are less apparent in second editions.

John knows that his relation to books is unique, as is that of any book-lover. His love has taken this form of hunting for first editions and for a deepening of the feeling they give him when, holding them at the moment of discovery, he is sensitive to their proper message and significance.

23 In Search of a Job

He had to choose among a number of different apprenticeships. His father and mother and the rest of the family made a number of suggestions one evening at the dinner table. Jim had not been so good at school and did not want to stay on beyond the minimum school leaving age. He wanted to become financially independent and to him it did not matter much what job he took. But his family cared, and everyone had an opinion about where the boy could be happy while earning a decent living. Trade Union practice would not permit more than so many apprentices in various trades and Jim could perhaps choose a blind alley if he was not careful.

Once as he was shopping for his mother he found himself in a grocery where the smells of spices and the display of bottles, tins and jars moved him to enquire whether there was a vacancy for an apprentice, instead of asking for the items on his list. The assistant was not quite sure how to take this. Instead of answering, she said: "Do you really want to be shut up in a shop like this all day? At your age?"

"I'd be in some other job anyway, and it might not be so interesting."

"What's so interesting about this place, then?"

"Don't you like the smells of spices, and all these cheeses, and so many things with exciting names—Hawaiian pineapples, Jamaican rum, French Camembert, sauerkraut, ravioli, Lapsang tea and so on. Just by moving from shelf to shelf I'd cover tremendous distances without even leaving the shop."

"Well, yes, if you look at it like that—but you know, there aren't only goods here, there are customers, too. Some of them are awful."

"But aren't there nice customers too?"

"'Course there are, but because they're nice, you don't seem to notice them. The others, you could break a bottle on their heads, just hearing their sarcastic voices when you're at the back looking for something special. At least, I'm like that: I have my likes and dislikes, don't you?"

Jim was going to answer when a young lady, well dressed and made up, came into the shop. Forgetting everything, Jim turned to her as if he had been on the staff and said: "Can I help you, Madam?" The lady answered by handing him her shopping list. Only then did Jim realize how difficult it would be for him to perform such a simple task. He would have to be guided about the shelves for days before he could put his hands at once on some of the lines that were not so much in demand. Jim passed the list to the assistant and stood aside thoughtfully. He had not realized that there must be principles of classification for the many hundreds of items displayed. Who had invented or discovered them? Were they used in all grocery shops? Would it be possible to improve upon them? How long would it take him to master this field and to become perhaps adviser to a big chain of groceries, in order to take advantage of the idea that had just come to him?

While Jim was thinking and dreaming, the owner of the shop came in from the back carrying a large crate full of tinned tuna fish which had just come in from Northern Spain. Although the owner had noticed a waiting customer, he did not leave what he was doing to go and serve her, but took the crate to where a gap appeared among the tinned fish. He did not arrange the tins to fill the gap but, putting the crate down, approached Jim instead: "Good morning; how are you today?"

Jim came back to his senses and said, "Oh, yes!—and how are you?"

"In this dreadful weather? Bearing up. What can I do for you?"

Jim looked at his shopping list and asked for two pounds of sugar and a pound of tea.

The young lady, carrying two loaded bags, was now ready to go. The proprietor of the shop went to open the door and thank her for calling. Wondering why he did not rush to help her with her load, Jim discovered that this new idea of his was so powerful that it cut him off from everybody and everything. All he wanted was to be alone at home to consider it more carefully and let it guide his life.

With his sugar and tea he left for home.

24 Selling Vegetables

It was two o' clock in the morning. Who could believe that this van was heading for Covent Garden, forty miles away? Still this was one of Reg's daily chores as owner of a small greengrocery shop north of the Thames. Reg always took the same route but it never was the same for the season, the weather, the person beside him, the state of the road—all contributed to making each journey a new one. Not forgetting the unpredictable behavior of this van which had perhaps done the journey a thousand times. Reg could never say which of his experiences had been the most fascinating. Was it the wet mornings, the smells of the fields at that hour, the faint dawn becoming a glorious sunrise, the play of the clouds or the shadows of the trees on the edge of the road; or was it the conversation he'd once had with a visiting Australian cousin who was amazed that Reg enjoyed getting up so early, working in the small hours, just to earn a living which did not seem so much better than his own in a comfortable job.

Reg cannot deny it is a hard life but he finds it an exciting and challenging way of making a living. When he travels alone he can concentrate on getting to London to pick up the kind of fruit and vegetables he knows his customers prefer and can afford. There are a number of hazards in this trade. These living things don't last for ever. Every evening he has to measure the amount he has to throw away because it is going bad, cannot be sold and would spoil the remaining produce. As he does this, he delicately assesses the chances of selling a slightly blemished fruit or vegetable; who among the buyers will accept it and who may feel hurt and complain.

To the latter, he will have to replace the goods for nothing, a sheer loss. How many lessons he has learnt this way! People are so different! His clientele includes a very wealthy retired couple who do their own shopping every day and enjoy feeling each apple or tomato they buy; an old maid who comes every day too, for a group of foreign students living in digs and cooking their evening meal themselves; a few bachelors, some tight-lipped and unsmiling, who come sometimes just for a lemon, sometimes for the most expensive and exotic fruit that Reg risks buying without knowing anything about it. He naturally has favorites among his customers, with whom from the start a very good relationship has developed. They trust Reg and never look at what he gives them, how he prices it or what his final bill is.

Reg has noticed that these people go with him in his mind to Covent Garden and help him choose and decide, as silent companions, when he is in doubt.

Naturally it is Reg who finally has the responsibility for what he takes home. His suppliers know him and have come to like him.

They understand something of the retail trade, though they themselves only deal as wholesalers with greengrocers or caterers. When Reg looks attentively at a crate containing some queer new produce, they see him considering in his heart the possible buy. They can sometimes hear him say: "Mr. Williams, would you like to try this strange and wonderful vegetable? I don't know a thing about it, but if it has been sent so far it must be good. Of course, it's expensive but it certainly makes a change, doesn't it?" Sometimes the suppliers hear him laugh aloud because in the imagined customer's reply Reg has been amazed to hear that Mr. Williams has for years eaten this vegetable cooked in twenty different ways in Brazil or Uganda or Pakistan.

For those who did not know Reg it seemed strange that one could love this trade above all other ways of earning a living. For Reg life was full, varied, rewarding in spite of the many risks involved, the frustrations of a bad season and the dock strikes that made him consider such lines as tinned or frozen food, thereby losing all the glamour of his trips to Covent Garden.

25 Shop People

The poor lift boy went up and down so often telling people what was sold on each floor and taking unknown customers on their unknown errands.

In this big store there were escalators as well as lifts. The store was usually crowded at some times of day and then the staff had a period of intense activity following periods of slackness. How they wished the public would arrange to come in a steady stream so that each customer could be served properly and not allowed to get angry if he was impatient. But the staff were called upon from all directions for different things—no wonder they got nervous if three or four people were waiting to be served.

People were attracted to this store because they could find almost anything they wanted, quality goods as well as everyday articles, at prices that were slightly lower than elsewhere. Regular customers came to know as well as the lift boy where to go for what, and sometimes developed a very friendly relationship with one or other of the sales staff.

Because of the public's queer habit of coming when it wanted, the sales people often had some time to gossip. Naturally gossiping about one's own colleagues is an immediate temptation. The staff forms a small community in which one has to choose one's friends, one's clothes, where one lives and so on with a certain care. Likes and dislikes cannot always be controlled and tension can be felt in some departments whether one comes for a small purchase or to place a big order. The supervisor may be dreaded or despised, a weakling appointed by a powerful friend or a tyrant kept there by a frightened manager. In some departments the customer is served politely and happily while in others he may see three people standing idly by each willing one of the others to come and serve him.

In the department selling sheets, towels and other household linen, the supervisor is a man and one of his chief assistants is a lady who, no longer young, has worked in the shop since it was founded. She has seen it grow in importance and popularity and believes that this is in part due to her. The supervisor, to avoid making the other staff jealous, treats this senior colleague with tact but also with firmness. Sometimes, to watch the two is as good as being in a theatre where two cunning actors are trying to out-do each other in such a way that nobody notices. Little do the pair know that their disagreements are the delight of the whole department and a talking point for the whole floor. Every morning when the lady reaches her counter, her colleagues look at her to assess her mood and the chances of seeing her reach the peak of tension within the limits of good manners, soft voices and apparent cordiality. If she comes in singing and cheerful all are disappointed since she will be well able to stand the supervisor's nagging and ordering about. If she comes in looking tired and tight-lipped they rejoice because today any hints or even slight double meanings will provide opportunities for blowing up.

There are other places in big stores where human problems can be found that are not suspected by the hasty customer.

26 At the Post Office

Charles once more found himself reaching the stamp counter just one second after a man got there. Charles only wanted one stamp to send a single letter but the man in front had a boxful of letters of different sizes, some that needed weighing, some stamping, some registering, and some to be sent express delivery. Charles had no change to get stamps from the machine; no other counter was open and the letter just had to be posted that day. Armed with patience, Charles stood watching the clerk at work. There were so many registered letters that the clerk ran out of receipts and had to fetch a new book from a locked cupboard behind him. Finding the key seemed to take ages, but at last the cupboard was opened. New carbon paper had to be extracted from a special box and inserted in the book. The registration went on. Some letters were to be sent to countries not familiar to the clerk, so consultation of the Post Office Guide was required. It was not always clear what the charge was and then the supervisor had to be called from behind his desk.

As time went on and the pile diminished, Charles felt that he would soon be served. But no, when all the letters had been weighed, entered in books, stamped and placed in a basket, the man drew out a long typed list of stamps of different values which he had been asked to buy.

Charles' heart sank and he looked once more in despair at the clock, which had advanced eighteen minutes since his arrival. It seemed that this next business might take just as long. His impatience was so obvious that the clerk looked at him with sympathetic but helpless eyes. The man in front turned round and said: "If you imagine that instead of me there was a long queue of people, each with one of my letters, you would not tend to get so impatient. In fact, you could consider me as many people rolled into one. I bring the Post Office good business while a one-letter man like you may cost more than he brings!"

Charles had never thought of this. It was true that he was only concerned with his bad luck, but this man was right—how could the Post Office work and provide a service without firms which sent so many letters and parcels at once?

Helped by these thoughts about the economics of the Post Office, he was just beginning to forget his bad luck when he saw that the clerk had run out of stamps of a particular value. So he had to go to his chief for more stamps and then sign a receipt when the chief had opened a safe and a portfolio to get them. Back at his place, he tore the sheet along the perforations, stuck the stamps in his book and from one of the smaller sheets counted out those the man wanted. Charles' luck was really out when the clerk found another empty page and had to go through the same process all over again.

It was just thirty-one minutes after reaching the window that Charles got his stamp. Behind him a queue had formed in no time and the clerk served over twenty people in less than five minutes. Charles watched him and timed it.

On his way home, Charles played the game of measuring his good luck by considering that there were only so many letters and not twice as many, only so few stamps missing and not all of them.

It was ironical to think that one has to be so unlucky in order to learn about work at the Post Office counter.

27 Expensive Meals

The war had just ended. Paris was slowly emerging from four years of hardship and want. It was difficult to find a place to eat where the food tasted as good as food before the war. Ersatz everywhere unless it was rutabaga or potatoes.

Overlooking the river Seine not far from Notre Dame there was a restaurant famous a hundred years ago as the meeting place of writers and poets and their friends or admirers. Then, because of its fame, the bohemians became excluded and the bourgeois were welcome. The restaurant soon changed hands and prices upped and upped. Between the two world wars it became 'l'endroit chic' where you would invite people you wanted to impress. The menu was among the top five in the whole of France. Unfortunately the only palates to taste the food were those of people whose purses were full.

A visitor to Paris in 1945 knowing anything of the history of French literary clubs and finding himself near the restaurant would feel so tempted to see this famous place. He would mount the four or five flights of stairs on foot—in those days the lifts could be used only at certain times of day—and . . . As you pushed the door open, a waiter would come and take your coat to the cloakroom (just for the tip you could get a whole meal elsewhere.) You and your friend were then led to a corner table, silver white, impeccably set and candle-lit, with newly-upholstered eighteenth-century style chairs. As you sat down you were given the wine list and your friend was handed a menu.

Visitors who had no idea of where their curiosity was leading them looked only at the prices, not the names of the dishes on the left. Embarrassed, unhappy, comparing their wealth with the cost of each course and recognizing that some dishes would require all their money and more, they would slowly get up, go quietly to the head waiter and try to explain as best they could that they had, well, come to the wrong place. Wrong, that is for the likes of them. An expression of contempt would flit across the head waiter's face as if he himself were one of the millionaires of the world and not their servant, a salaried man who knows there are other places where one can eat to suit one's pocket.

He would open the door as if to throw the unfortunate visitors out, forgetting the coats. If asked for them, he would call the attendant and tell her: "Give these gentlemen their coats" adding: "Don't expect a tip, they have no money yet they expect to eat at the most famous restaurants!"

Some visitors never consider that all this would not have happened had they been less naïve and better informed. They feel the head waiter has no manners and should not have embarrassed them as he did. Once out on the street, they enquire for a cheap restaurant not too far away.

A few steps down a narrow and winding side-street, two or three restaurants, far less inviting, announce menus at prices that may be afforded. The four-course traditional meal of the French is still on but the quantity and quality of what is offered remind one of the reality of France's shortage and the valiant attempt to preserve appearances at all cost. Even the famous French bread is scarcely more than a memory; one slice is all you are allowed, when bread was always unlimited in French restaurants. The single radish that goes with the single olive and an atom of butter to form the hors d'oeuvre augurs badly for the subsequent entrée, plat de résistance and dessert. Indeed *you* can believe you have eaten—but not your stomach.

Perhaps at the end it costs as much proportionately as it would at the famous restaurant.

28 Stranded

The bad weather had closed all airports in the area. The nearest sizeable one open was about a hundred miles away and all planes were re-directed towards it.

For the city, this meant finding hotel accommodation for several hundred stranded passengers. Each airline got busy booking rooms for its own passengers. The competition was keen that week for large conferences had already made space very short. Passengers already annoyed at having to change plans, at queuing for telephones to call their homes, their business contacts or both, were impatient with the airline personnel for not doing what only fairies do in children's tales.

The airport staff had experience of such mishaps. They had forecast the influx of aircraft and knew what to do to appear highly prepared for such occasions. On the loudspeakers their voices seemed calm and firm, giving clear instructions to passengers and expecting to be obeyed quietly by all, young or old, tired or not-so-tired.

But even they lost heart when plane after plane was made to land at the airport and hordes of passengers were thrust on them with no sign of a solution to the lodging problem. From time to time a new idea would be tried out with an announcement over the loudspeakers: 'Passengers wishing to go by sleeper to such-and-such a destination should see so-and-so at such-and-such a counter . . . Buses and coaches are available to take passengers to X and intermediary stops on route Y! . . . Through the kind co-operation of the city's tourist organization it has been possible to find homes ready to accommodate single ladies for the night!'

In the hotels queues formed at the reception desks. So many haggard faces; women with babies, who could not be given priority in the circumstances since nobody was prepared to be completely stranded in an unknown place; families of four who accepted to share a double room—all indicating the irony of expected quick travel in reasonable comfort and the actual waste of a day or so in very different conditions.

The worst element in all this was the grudge passengers bore the airlines and their staffs. Surely "they" knew before take-off what the weather conditions were; but "they" still herded them into the planes to a wrong destination and hardships which were not in the program. Very few saw what was happening as a blessing compared with the risk of a forced landing or a landing at an airport thousands of miles away with no facilities at all and no personnel with any experience of such emergencies.

Travelers who had been in similar circumstances would recount them to their bored companions or compare them with this night, blaming their rescuers for such or such an administrative weakness.

Very occasionally, laughter would be heard and a joke made to calm spirits would be well received by tired people whose sense of humor had not altogether gone to sleep.

29 A Visit to the Doctor

It was decided to take the children to the child specialist. An appointment had been made a few days earlier for 9 a.m. but the busy doctor could give his time only as it was available, not according to the appointments book. So the parents waited for over half an hour before being shown into the consulting room.

The waiting room had seats for children of different ages and for their parents. There were a few plastic toys on a low table and under it a cradle in which there was a doll under a blanket.

The older child, a girl, picked up one of the toys and said, "There's nothing underneath." She meant that the toys being hollow and placed on the table on their wider base, they suggested to her places which some little creatures lived in. But this was not the case: the toys had really very little to offer except perhaps as something to chew, so she turned round and examined each chair, stool and settee, remarking on their smoothness, their design and their similarity or otherwise to those at home.

At length the family was called in and a nurse started filling in forms: the girl's name, age, father's name, occupation, address, National Health Card, National Insurance number and so on. Then the procedure was repeated for the other child, a baby boy, while the specialist was busy talking to his staff and giving a telephone consultation.

The infra-red heaters above the couch were switched on. The mother undressed the baby while the doctor filled in a few more details he needed on the form. Then the whole family gathered round the baby with the doctor. The examination started. First, hand palpation, expert hands manipulating a seemingly fragile body. No cries. Here and there a mental note; the child will need this or that, but perhaps time will do the job better. From time to time a word to the parents to indicate interest in them and to share what may well have been their preoccupation. He took the stethoscope and listened carefully to the rhythms of vital parts, and then said abruptly: "Dress him now."

While he was being dressed the doctor went back to his desk, jotted down some notes and considered in quick succession the various questions about the baby and his mother's worries. He wrote a number of suggestions about feeding, looking after the usual ailments and preventing others, noting dates for vaccination. Then he said, "Would you undress the girl," and asked points concerning the child's medical history. Had she already had measles, whooping cough, chicken pox etc? When had she been vaccinated and against what diseases?

When all this had been recorded, the doctor examined the girl thoroughly and made his recommendations.

The visit had been a long one and other patients had arrived at the clinic, crowding the waiting room. The nurses were busy explaining the delays, feeling the doctor could perhaps have finished with this new family a little earlier.

A new appointment was fixed for a month ahead.

On their way out the parents did not exchange views on the doctor's examination, but only about their children and what his recommendations meant. Some unasked questions occurred to them: was it wiser to ring the doctor and rely on his memory of the case or to wait till the next visit and put the question to him then if it was still relevant? The anxious mother was for immediate enquiry, while the reluctant father sought excuses not to call again so soon. How urgent was it? Would it be only to put their minds at rest or was it vital to have this opinion now? The tension within was growing for it did not seem that the father summed up the situation as fairly and directly as the mother.

By the time they reached home a compromise had been reached. They would start the treatment at once and call the doctor if they noticed any signs of the suspected trouble. Since most people go to the doctor as much for comfort as for treatment, the visit had fulfilled its purpose.

30 To Have a Garden

"It's so lovely to have a garden!" cried Mrs. Smith who had called for a chat with Mrs. Johnson. "Yes isn't it?" answered her hostess, "When the flowers are out and the colors mix so well, you really feel proud of your work. Does your husband help in the garden? Mine does, he loves to plant out the flower beds and he's always looking for something new."

"I wish Will were like that," said Mrs. Smith, "he does nothing till he feels ashamed in front of the neighbors, then he gets out the mower and mows the front lawn with terrific energy. But he gets tired in a quarter of an hour, his hands get sore and blistered; the fact is, he leaves it all to me and you know what it is to have a house to run and a family to look after. If you add the garden, life really becomes a burden."

"Why doesn't Mr. Johnson find it relaxing?"

"I wish I knew. He's healthy, fairly strong, loves beautiful things and is ever so keen on nature generally but he says gardening's a specialist's job and it so happens he's specialized in something else."

"I've always thought there's nothing more pleasant to do around the house than to look after the garden," said Mrs. Smith; "at least there your work and your tastes show. You cook for hours and the meals are swallowed in a few minutes: you clean the house and dust has settled again before you've finished. But plant a seed or a bulb or a shoot and everyday you feel the working of nature and the mystery of growing things that become more yours the more you tend them. And it makes you interested in what other people are doing. Gives you more to talk about than 'how are you?' or the weather. You get to know so much about soils, keeping the goodness in the earth by adding fertilizers. You find out about pruning and where you put various flowers to grow best or to give the best effect."

"I'm just like you, Mrs. Smith, I love to work in the garden, but it doesn't help at all to think that your husband is indoors enjoying a concert while you break your back digging up weeds. Now there's a thankless task for you! Wasting your time and energy while he could have done it so well and easily. But there's nothing doing, he won't hear of it when it's a matter of the garden. Mind you, he's most helpful round the house. It is only where the garden is concerned that we don't see eye-to-eye. He just has no interest in what fascinates you and me and so many others."

"Perhaps it's a special allergy. Can't you take him to a psychiatrist for this?"

"What, do you think it can be a phobia, or some mental trouble that keeps him away from a garden?"

"Maybe."

"I can't believe that. I prefer to think of it as the freedom to choose one's activities and for my husband gardening just comes bottom of the list."

"Perhaps you're right, Mrs. Johnson, but it would have been so nice for you if your husband could be sharing your interest in flowers and gardens. Try again, there may be some way—going to flower shows, leaving gardening magazines about, visiting parks at the peak of the season?"

"Something like that might do the trick; but perhaps I prefer to toil harder in the garden and leave him alone. Thanks very much for calling, Mrs. Smith. Goodbye."

"Goodbye Mrs. Johnson—and all the best."

31 Tragic Holiday

The man met his death by drowning.

The return trip was very sad as his family had to get his body back to their home town. In the convoy were his widow and his two children, his friends and also the dog who seemed to feel the grief more than anyone.

It had happened during the holiday. The family undertook a long trip to reach a warm and quiet beach where for two weeks they would really be away from their strenuous occupations. They had so looked forward to this vacation and a real long family get-together after months of brief, tired encounters.

The place they had found was ideal from every point of view. Everyone was as happy as could be, running on the soft sand, splashing in the shallow water, sunbathing, building sand-castles, playing volley-ball and racing each other in the water and along the shore. The refreshing sea-breeze would cool them after the more hectic games.

One day they were tempted to try a new part of the beach, where the heavy surf looked so inviting. The high waves broke so majestically upon the sand, challenging the bathers to take them at the crest and feel the water's drop on every one of their muscles.

But the little dog became restless and started barking and growling as if he wanted to stop the whole project. Nobody paid any attention to him, all felt he was a thorough nuisance, yet he became still more insistent, pressing against his mistress' legs and pushing the little girl back from the water's edge. To calm him down, the mother and daughter stayed behind; but the dog was still not content, he went on barking and warning the boy and the two men were who already in the ocean up to their waists.

The spot was treacherous, but as the beach was not yet popular, nobody had put up a sign to warm swimmers. Soon it became evident that the big waves created an undercurrent which, acting on the sand, caused a huge drag on the bathers' legs and made them lose their balance.

The threat was so suddenly felt and so clearly menacing that the three swimmers panicked and at once tried clumsily to reach firm ground. The boy seemed the most agile and managed to find enough strength for his fight against the current, the inrushing waves and that much more destroying element—the fear that saps one's courage. The friend struggled and struggled, swallowing mouthfuls of horrible salty water, raising his head again above the waves, seeing the beach almost within reach, only to sink once more. Suddenly feeling the sand under his feet, he managed with the help of a threatening wave to drag himself out of danger.

From the shore the woman, her daughter and the dog stared aghast at the third victim. He was a strong swimmer, an active man who enjoyed taking risks. But now he cried desperately for help as he was tossed up and down on the choppy surface with nothing to hang onto except the faint hope of outside help. The back-current was strong, will-power and his efforts were in vain and the struggle ceased with the final plunge to the bottom.

It took three-quarters of an hour for a rescue team to find his body and bring it back to the shore.

32 The Highway Code

How much easier things were when it was possible to sit at the wheel of a car and learn to drive with no test and no need to prove oneself except by keeping safe on the roads. The roads were incomparably less good than nowadays, but there were fewer cars and one could drive carefree. Today, road users of all kinds must not only be skilled at the wheel, but need to know about insurance, the law and their rights and duties.

The Highway Code is far from definitive. New discoveries in technology, higher demands from commerce, more people on the roads and more interest in travel produce new circumstances that call for the renewal of the traffic regulations. It becomes daily more imperative that no one should be allowed on the roads who is a menace to other road users.

It is simple logic that drivers should learn to become masters of any vehicle they may drive in circumstances as varied as life itself. It is also logical for them to know the meaning of all the road signs and the rules for road behavior.

To the first end, practice is given to the learner under the guidance of an expert driver who has some means of avoiding the dangers beginners must meet or cause. Driving-school cars nearly always have dual controls. L-plates on the car warn road users that an unskilled driver is at the controls and that they should take extra care.

Rarely do beginners manage their cars properly without practice. There are so many simultaneous requirements involving the driver's feet, hands, eyes and mind, that very often the first feeling is one of chaos. Jerks, sudden halts, swerves are all so common that instructors expect them as the mark of all beginners. It is however clear that almost anyone can learn to master a motor vehicle, so to accept that beginners will inevitably cause chaos can be seen as a pre-conceived idea on the part of the instructor. It may be short-sightedness which teachers with a different sensitivity could correct. No doubt, beginners would be less tense and less of a menace to others on the roads if instructors could be less pragmatic and cynical and more sensitive to what learners bring with them.

One expects the Highway Code to be learned in the same way that factual knowledge is assimilated in school. In fact, except for some arbitrariness in a few road signs, it is possible to see the logic in traffic rules. Most are seen to be common sense when one considers them, though different countries apply a few experimental rules in order to learn the value of some idea. These rules are kept in the Code for a year or two till evidence contradicts a suggestion or confirms its soundness.

As tourists, people are allowed to break the minor rules that are not universal, but when they settle in a country they must take the test again to prove to the traffic authorities that they are familiar with every aspect of the local Highway Code. An International license covers one only as a visitor to a country— even if the visit is prolonged for several months. There seems to be need for more local experimentation before all countries accept one single Highway Code. Naturally, until all countries adopt the same rule of the road, as regards driving on the left or right for example, it will be difficult to establish a universal Code. Other obstacles are the presence of high mountains in one land when there are none in others; the tendency in some countries to keep fast roads through built-up areas whilst in others motorways avoid town-centers wherever possible; the preference for powerful cars and speedy traffic; congestion or lack of it in cities; different levels of road development. Nevertheless, most countries are now beginning to adopt an international set of road signs.

Flexibility of the mind, adaptability to cars, roads, rules of traffic, must necessarily be increased if a driver is to be a good and safe one.

33 The Spirit of Music

The music teacher had a good method, people used to say. He would make his pupils play some easy tunes straight away and then learn technique, scales and score-reading incidentally.

In fact, this teacher's success came from different sources. He was much more concerned with his pupils as people than with his own theory of music teaching. So he would start with each in a different way until he discovered how the pupil's gifts could form a springboard for all that followed. This seemed sound teaching and gave each and all a feeling of receiving the maximum of attention and help from the teacher.

"Music," the teacher would tell his pupils, "is a state of being. It is not so much knowledge and know-how. If you want to be good at playing an instrument, let music get hold of you first and this will turn get hold of your muscles and make them produce the music that is now inside you. How can music come *out* of an instrument if it is not first put *into* it? And who is to put it there?

The composer, the maker of the instrument, the printed score or the player?"

This usually helped the pupils to understand and they would start by trying to discover what it is to have music inside one, only afterwards learning how to express its various facets.

Naturally, for most pupils, singing and humming indicated that there was music within ready to be brought out. But before this stage there was need to listen and to evoke tunes, melodies, harmonizations, etc. The first instrument was therefore one's self, which can serve to enlighten the searching mind in quest of music and which can be used in complex manners.

One's self is very complex indeed; no wonder that by returning to it we find so much we need in order to understand music.

One can acquire music by listening. Listening truly is to open up, to surrender to sound and let it mould whatever is available for this in the self. But at the same time, the self has means of showing that it has something to express. So music comes out of the singer or the hummer only when evocation has allowed him to recognize that it is adequate. All this is clearly fundamental for learners of music as well as for teachers, and that is why it served our teacher's purpose so well.

Musical instruments are extensions of the awareness of how music is manifested in a self, and learning to play them involves entering the particular form of music held in each. To know an instrument is only possible *via* the music which it was built to play. Learning the instrument is the process of intimacy that tells one what to do, and how, in order to stimulate a response from it. This is followed by a growing intimacy that steers the user towards getting more and more from himself through it, while getting more and more from it through himself. Without this process of mutual intimacy, neither the player nor the instrument are concerned with music but only with gestures and sounds that correspond to each other abstractly.

Because of one's surrender, one can receive. Because one has received, one can return, and to understand this process it is not necessary to consider whole melodies or tunes. Even from the simplest tunes one can recognize its existence and significance.

Bringing this vision to his pupils, the music teacher devised a number of techniques to use with a number of instruments which people wanted to play. The soundness of the approach made all the pupils aware of the music in themselves, and that they could make it obvious to others through the instrument after it had been made obvious to them in their own flesh. Others saw only the outer manifestations of the vision and they would talk of it as an old, unfashionable way of going about things.

Everyday, the teacher gave thanks for his understanding of how the spirit moved him to know where to look for the essentials of music.

34 Life in the Country

The hazards of nature are best known by those who live in the country. It is one thing to seek shelter in a shop in a hailstorm and another to tour one's property and reckon the damage afterwards. It is one thing to take a walk on a sunny day and quite another to pray for dry weather to ripen the crops.

City dwellers are becoming so numerous that fewer and fewer people can imagine what it is like to live near to nature, to be regulated by natural events, to be surrounded by the mysteries of the seasons and feel the pulse of time. It is far from enough to read about nature, to camp occasionally, to travel around by car. Life in the country such as farmers live is as distinct as can be from life in towns and cities.

Of course, everyone can see this sociologically. There are so many different ways of being entertained in a city outside office or factory hours. There are few distractions on a farm and the hours of work are as long as daylight.

Still, the main differences lie somewhere else. Country life is demanding and calls for many skills. One has to be a jack-of-all trades to cope with numerous emergencies and with the varying needs of the moment for, except on the largest farms, it is not easy to enlist the help of a specialist for each breakdown in machinery, plumbing or electricity. It is not possible to put off jobs on the land if the weather is going to change.

Rhythms of plant growth and the mere fact that things are different every day force each mind into a state of expectation, of suspense which in the city, only people in creative jobs know. If there are animals on the farm, yet another dimension is added.

True, many people do not like life in the country. They object to the smells, the irregularities of everyday programs, and leave the land to settle in towns. At one time, not to leave the family farm was considered either as a weakness of character or as a sign that one would inherit the property. To stay was in the latter case to secure a future, while for those who would not become the owners it was to reject adventure and the unknown.

Again we move from human experience to sociology. In fact, peasants or farm laborers who move to towns have little real knowledge of city life before they leave the land. They may have dreamed of it. Once facing facts, the foremost need is employment, to do anything even as an unskilled worker in the most routine job. If the result is more money, this is the positive side that is stressed: hence new city-dwellers are at once forced to see materialistic considerations as the only ones worth bothering about.

City dwellers are often so used to their comforts that they believe losing them means a drop in human status. But why can we not measure civilization's progress in terms of life's obvious features? Nowadays comforts can be bought and then people are often frightened at the mere thought of losing them. Those who have not known them are considered primitive, inferior.

Can't we say something similar about the loss every one of us experiences when we can no longer be sensitive to what, for centuries, have been gifts to man? The fashion of camping, or taking summer cottages, can be seen as a withdrawal from city-life into nature, but a withdrawal by town dwellers who like to feel others near them in large numbers before letting nature enter their sensitivities. Nature's pull exists and is proof of man's recognition that he is of the same stuff as nature. But the resistances exist too.

Everyone's education could include a direct study of what he is most: a product of nature as we know it on Earth, a free being who chooses individually whether to link with others and institutions or with the universe at large.

35 Future Tourists

They had saved for years in order to go on a long holiday together. While they had little money, there was no point in looking at maps or visiting travel agents. They got so used to saving for something in the distant future that they stopped keeping count and suddenly found themselves with twice as much money as their original target; enough for a trip anywhere. Now they could indeed choose and for once money was no problem.

But how does one choose where to go?

Their neighbors had tastes they would not agree with. So there was no point in asking their advice, except perhaps on how to get the best value for their money. The advertisements they saw made everywhere look attractive from a distance, but they had heard and read enough stories to make them at least cautious before taking an advertisement at its face value. So the man went to the bookshop, bought maps and a few travel books and some guides and came home laden with information.

"We shall have to do some reading," said he, spreading out on the table the results of his shopping.

"We may have to plan our reading, otherwise we'd spend our holiday reading rather than travelling," said she.

"That might not be such a bad idea after all this time at home and in the garden."

"Surely we've saved to go on a trip and that's what I'm going to do before I die. Let's have a look at these books and maps."

She chose Europe and he South America. They spread out their maps and silently scanned all these lands open to them if they cared to visit them. In her map of Europe, the colors indicated that there were many countries and that going to some meant going through many others. This attracted her, particularly when she looked at Italy and Greece, these lands of ancient civilizations with so much treasure inviting one to visit them.

On his map, the countries were many too, but he suspected that distances were much greater than in Europe and that therefore days would be spent in travelling from place to place. Moreover, much of South America is for explorers, not tourists like them. Mountains, equatorial forests were so plentiful that for someone with an adventurous mind there would be no question of going elsewhere. Perhaps though, looking South near Santiago de Chile and Buenos Aires or Montevideo, one would find a number of cities attractive for several reasons. Now he saw what to suggest from this point of view if he was to be the first to voice an opinion.

He raised his head and saw that his wife had gone to her armchair and was avidly reading a guide to Greece. On her lap was spread one of Italy. He was glad, for these two countries had taken first place in his unspoken wishes, though he did not want to influence her. Now there would be real agreement and they would spend their time preparing for the trip itself, rather than in making a choice. However much these attractive books had cost, nothing could compare with the first-hand experience which awaited the couple. So now he could plan tickets, reservations, timetables, insurance and the buying of equipment for the trip. All this he knew would give him pleasure now and prepare him for the pleasure to come.

"Where do you think, dear?" he asked.

"I think we should go to Greece, but what have you found out?"

"I'm so glad, because I vote for Greece too."

"Don't you think that's too quick a decision: there may be better ways of spending our savings."

"As far as I'm concerned Greece will fulfill most of our dreams if the trip's well planned and we're lucky with the weather."

"Even though I think we ought to spend a few days looking at all this stuff, I am very much inclined to choose Greece and see its skies and ruins."

"We shall read all these books when we come home. It's only a few weeks, anyway."

"Let's."

36 Waiting

The old man stood in a queue to get his pension. There were a number of old age pensioners in front of him. He was tired and sad and would have preferred to stay in bed today. But it is the rule of the country that he has to present himself personally on a certain day to prove he is entitled to his pension.

As the queue advanced and he came closer to the paying officer, his thoughts went from himself to her. For some years now he had come every week to this same office. A number of officers had worked there before she arrived, but she seemed to love it so much that the pensioners got an extra fillip in being served by her. Without holding up the queue she would ask everyone by name how he or she was, what were the effects of some recently prescribed medicine, how the good or bad weather was affecting body and spirits. She knew exactly when to stop so that no one felt neglected while others were pampered. Her secret was to get the next two or three people in the queue interested in the conversation. Sometimes they were so moved that they would volunteer to give a hand to a stranger in front of them in the queue.

When our old man reached her window he was determined this week not to fall into the trap of her sympathy for himself and for others.

"Good morning, Mr. Brown. You look rather pale this morning. Is there anything I can do for you now besides paying your pension?"

"Thank you, Miss. I prefer to keep my worries to myself rather than worry everybody else with them. Besides, you mustn't allow yourself to be taken up in helping so many sad and decrepit old people. We're bound to get worse, that is, older, every week. You must think of yourself before you get to be like us."

"I don't agree, Mr. Brown, nor do the other people behind you in this very queue, I should think."

"Hear, hear!" said a few voices, echoing the girl's opinion.

"Well, I didn't intend to start a discussion, I just think it's sad for anybody to grow old and lonely."

"In a way, yes; but perhaps it's simply an error of judgment. Perhaps we all need education in growing old. It's inevitable. Perhaps if the surprise of meeting what is in store disappeared,

132

we might all learn to enjoy every period of our life as we enjoy childhood and youth."

"That's easily said. I used to walk for miles and enjoy the smells of the woods—now I can hardly stand up for half an hour in this queue. I'll feel all my joints aching for two days at least. I'd very much like to enjoy my rheumatism, but it's simply impossible!"

"Of course there's a difference between youth and old age, but my idea is that we get a shock in growing old, while we could be enjoying the newness of a life when we're free to think, contemplate, feel sympathy, reflect on our own foolishness and that of our friends! Old age has a purpose, even if we've not found it yet. It certainly does not mean regretting that we are no longer young. Don't you think so?"

"Well, I need to start my re-education at the age of eighty by taking home your beautiful logic and finding out where I lost my grip on life. Do you know I will, I promise, and as the weeks go by I'll let you know how I'm getting on. Goodbye, Miss—and thank you."

"Do you agree with me, Mrs. Jones."

"Oh, yes; and I must say I enjoyed your lecturing Mr. Brown. He's a darling, but so stubborn in his thinking. Goodbye, Miss, till next week."

www.ingramcontent.com/pod-product-compliance
Lightning Source LLC
LaVergne TN
LVHW061224060426
835509LV00012B/1418

9 780878 252220